Val Proctor

SPIRITUAL UNFOLDMENT 4

Other books of White Eagle's teaching

SPIRITUAL UNFOLDMENT

4

The Path to the Light

WHITE EAGLE

THE WHITE EAGLE PUBLISHING TRUST

NEW LANDS · LISS · HAMPSHIRE · ENGLAND

White Eagle speaks through the instrumentality
of Grace Cooke

First published November 1988

© The White Eagle Publishing Trust, 1988

British Library CIP data

White Eagle *(Spirit)*
Spiritual Unfoldment.
4 : The path to the light
I. Title
133.9'3

ISBN 0-85487-078-4

*Set in 12 on 14pt Linotron Baskerville by
Goodfellow & Egan Phototypesetting Ltd, Cambridge
and printed in Great Britain at
the University Printing House, Oxford
by David Stanford
Printer to the University*

CONTENTS

PREFACE

THIS BOOK is a collection of White Eagle's teachings, given over many years, on the theme of following the way of brotherhood, 'the path to the light'. The first five chapters are drawn from a series of inner teachings given at consecutive meetings and although we have occasionally changed the sequence we have kept White Eagle's own title and called them 'The Path I', 'II', and so on. They form the first part of the book. The other teachings develop the same theme, and we have ended with a collection of shorter passages of encouragement and wisdom for the brother or sister on the path.

The beginning of the first teaching gives a little glimpse of the meetings at which they were all given. After a piece of recorded music – in this case the Good Friday music from Wagner's *Parsifal* – White Eagle would begin with a prayer which helped to lead the consciousness of his hearers away from the tumult of the outer world. Then he would normally greet them, and draw attention to the many spirit friends and angelic beings who were present. We have spoken of these meetings and where they took place in the preface to the third volume in the series.

We wish all who read these teachings lasting happiness.

THE PATH I

Our Father–Mother God, may we feel Thy sweet blessing in our hearts and in our lives; and may we, with Thy strength and Thy grace, have the power and the wisdom to radiate the light and truth of the Spirit. May the revelation of Thy holy mysteries gradually permeate our consciousness; and may we be patient as we walk the path of spiritual evolution, so that in due course we may understand the deep purpose of Thy plan. And in Thy name we call upon the angels of wisdom and love to bless this meeting.

Amen.

IT IS GOOD to be with you once again. We hesitate to spoil the beauty of the vibrations with the human voice. We do not know if you feel as we do, raised to an ecstasy by the music. We sometimes wish we could sing to you instead of speaking. In the old times, much of our work was done in this way, but

———

we are not going to talk about these things tonight. Will you give us your attention and your love? For we would speak about the mystical experiences which are the lot of every soul. We all, as individuals, pass through these soul-experiences; and although we are not always able to speak of them or describe them, sometimes we catch a glimpse of the eternal light of the heavenly glory, and experience the bliss of that heavenly place which is our true home. It is of little use forming some definite plan for development of spiritual powers, for every soul's experience is unique. This is why we feel that mistakes are sometimes made by beloved brethren endeavouring to bring all their acquaintances and friends onto one particular path.

We will call this series of talks 'The Path', and shall work from the birth of the soul, along the age-long path of human experience; and we shall, in due course, come to the meaning of initiation, for we see that many are still confused about initiation, and indeed about the whole process of spiritual growth and development.

No-one can say that any one path is the right path. The way he follows depends entirely on the individual soul; on experience gained in previous incarnations, and on karma which has been made. For this karma has to be worked out on a certain path, and everyone has to follow his or her individual path of training. The light shines through many differently-shaped and coloured windows, but eventually all colours are blended into the one ray, the Great White Light.

Let us get this quite clear; we must follow our particular path steadfastly and one-pointedly, but our work is not necessarily our neighbour's, nor is his work ours. It is essential that we get this broad outlook, this realisation that each path is good, according to the level of consciousness and the karma of the individual who follows it, and according to the needs of the general plan for the spiritual evolution of humanity.

We would emphasise the point that spiritual training goes much deeper than the mind, and also that to be of any lasting value it must become a way of life, an actual part of the life of the neophyte. A man or woman may have a remarkable intellectual knowledge of music, but intellectual knowledge does not necessarily make a musician. In the

same way, the development of the intellectual aspect of man's being is useful because it
enables him, in due time, to comprehend the
magnificence of God's universe; but occult
knowledge does not necessarily make a
master. It is rather striking that the stories of
the lives of masters and saints nearly all
indicate that those illumined ones have ever
been simple men and women, laying no
claim to great earthly knowledge. The life of
Jesus of Nazareth emphasises this, although
occult records reveal that he absorbed deep
knowledge from wise men, and also that his
purity and gentleness carried its own power
to centres of wisdom and learning in the
East, so badly needing at that time the purification of the Christ spirit.

At the present time many are eagerly
searching for knowledge; they are developing the mental body. This is all in the process
of evolution, a stage on the path. But it is not
sufficient to know things with the mind, for
such a knowing can be very limited. Spiritual
growth results from the soul absorbing and
digesting spiritual truth and putting into
practice the simple spiritual laws in daily life.
All depends upon the sincerity and purity of
the inner life, and the soul's response to the

finer vibrations of the heavenly worlds. It is no doubt entertaining and stimulating to read opinions of others, but your experience is unique to yourself. Do remember this.

Those who are drawn to the White Eagle Lodge come because they desire simplicity. Some may feel that the teaching given here is not sufficiently advanced, but this thought is prompted by an appetite for indigestible food. This is a natural bodily instinct, for the brain is of the body. We do not wish to offend, but we do want you to try to see where this desire for ever more intellectual and indigestible food is leading. It is not good to rush forward to gain inner secrets before the simple truths have been assimilated and *lived*. If we attempt to do so we come up against a sharp-edged tool, which will hurt us. Illumination and subsequent initiation come not through earthly knowledge but through spiritual experience. The daily response to God, to good, the practice of reception from the heavenly state, this is the only way of spiritual growth.

We have seen many passing through bitter human experiences, and sometimes the question arises: 'Why does not our guide interfere? Why does he not save us from

---

making mistakes? Why are we allowed to do foolish things and to suffer, when our spirit guide could have prevented us? Had we only known, we should not have done so and so'. It is natural to want to know what is coming along, especially with the idea that if only we knew, we could avoid certain pitfalls – for it is more comfortable to make a detour round a pond than to fall in. But if dropping into the pond is going to teach you to swim, if dropping into a spiritual pond is going to bring you illumination, or give you something beautiful – well! do not take that comfortable path round the pond!

We mean that to tread the path faithfully, you must be prepared to go through dark places as well as sunlit ones. You do not want to dodge obligations, or resent difficult happenings, but rather say, 'If I have to do this, well, let me get on with it!'. Be tranquil and courageous! Even if it is a little uncomfortable, do not try to escape your obligations, nor to evade the sorrows and disappointments of human life. They come to you as opportunities.

We talk about good and evil. What is the difference? Both alike are teachers.

The soul of man starts on its age-long

path of development when it begins its life in physical matter. The soul is born with the first putting through of the life of the spirit into physical manifestation. We are speaking of the soul, not the divine spark – which lives long before the soul is born. Then the soul is as a tiny babe, and for many lives remains a child, treading the path under guidance and with the help of those in charge. Then there comes a time when it passes from childhood into man- or womanhood, and sees for the first time the light which is to guide it further along the path. With the seeing of the light great responsibility comes. Whereas before the soul walked in ignorance and darkness, now it sees the path which lies before it, it becomes conscious of its path. As soon as it becomes conscious of its path a responsibility is laid upon it. Then it starts to work in earnest. The one who rejects his responsibility, who turns his back on the light he has once seen, endures sorrow, because to do so breaks a divine law.

Now when a soul first consciously sets out upon this path, trials and tests come – sorrows, problems, difficulties, and for a time all seems confusion. Although he is striving so hard to do right, the man feels as though he is in a fog; he finds himself up against people, and human problems, and then spiritual difficulties come crowding in, until he knows not which way to turn, or what to do. It is then that the temptation comes to throw everything over. 'I am sick and tired of this striving; I was far better just living in the outer world.' This is the moment of choice when you must resolve to 'keep on keeping on', quietly, and in complete trust and faith in God's love, for as Jesus himself said, *Ye know neither the day nor the hour when the Son of man cometh.* You know not from hour to hour what glorious experience will be yours, what great awakening will come. Tonight you may be in darkness, but tomorrow you could be illumined. When you reach the true home of the spirit, then will come peace, tranquillity, joy, and you will walk faithfully and quietly on the path upon which your feet are set.

This temptation we have described comes to all, though the individual experience is unique. The lesson each soul must learn is common to all humanity, although it may be presented to the individual soul in unique form. You cannot learn from your brother's experience, nor he from yours; neither can you fully understand another's experiences until you yourself have undergone them. Every soul has to face the same problems, to learn the same lessons; but your experiences are unique in so far as you learn them in a different set of circumstances, and therefore they can never be quite the same as your neighbour's.

You get impatient and exclaim, 'Oh, I cannot understand why Mr So-and-So does this, that or the other!'. But do try to remember that all are of God, all are of the same substance, and all are passing through difficulties and trials and temptations, even as you are. Send out your love and goodwill to all. You may think, 'This sounds very childish; we do not want to hear this over and over again!'. But these things are the very essence of spiritual evolution, of the mystical path which all must tread on their way to the Temple of the Great White Light, or the Temple of the Grail.

Divine Spirit, we are thankful to Thee for all that is beautiful and progressive and lovely in our lives. May we never forget Thy love, nor our brother's need for Thy love. We pray to become

―――

more worthy channels through which Thy light may shine in the darkened places of life.

Amen.

❦

⁕

2

THE PATH II

---

*Let us open our hearts to the love and wisdom of
the Eternal Spirit, from Whom we come and in
Whom we live; Who is omniscient, omnipotent,
omnipresent . . .*

Amen.

THE OMNIPRESENCE and the omniscience of
the eternal spirit is a comforting realisation.
The soul breathed forth from God always
retains that parental link; when we can
return again into the fuller consciousness of
this sustaining life, then we enter the eternal
peace.

In the process of the soul's growth it
strives to shake itself free, it seeks for freedom. Let us compare the child soul of a man
with the physical life of a child. We see in
that child the struggles for self-expression,
for self-will. It will cry and scream sometimes, and show its determination to get its

---

own way; and the wiser parent will give the child freedom to kick and shout and expand its lungs – but only up to a point. Then the child feels the strength and warmth of the parent, and although it may struggle and protest, in time it becomes docile and nestles against the heart of its parent. Thus they grow together, and the child absorbs wisdom from its parent. All that is most beautiful and most sweet in the parental plant can be transmitted to the child, and the fruits of later years become more sweet and mellow.

So it is with the child of God. There comes a time when the child comes to know and to trust the love and wisdom of its Father–Mother God; then the child no longer rebels, for it knows that God is all wisdom and the divine plan is perfect.

Let us picture the child on the path of spiritual evolution, sent forth by the Father–Mother God to dwell in form in the higher worlds, a Christlike form, truly created in God's image. Then we see this child of God descending through the higher spheres of life, down into densest matter. When the child first leaves its home it is very much of the heaven world, but from its first contact with the life on the physical plane, it begins

---

to weave its soul garment. In the beginning the young soul was perhaps more open, more receptive to the influence of the teachers from the higher realms. But as it descended and clothed itself more completely in denser garments, the spirit within became more shut in, the senses more obtuse, and so it was unable to respond to the higher worlds. In this state we see man in prison, bound and blindfolded – a condition in which he may remain through many incarnations.

This may appear terrible to those who do not understand, because it seems that the soul, bound to the wheel of rebirth, has no freedom, no opportunity. You may look out and think you see thousands of souls thus blindfolded and bound upon the wheel. But *we* see, beneath the bonds and the blindness, a beautiful process slowly taking place. We see a light – so masked and dimmed, but light it is! – within this form. We watch the journey through the ages, and see the soul passing through difficult earthly experiences. But we see too that in each life, light is absorbed. It may be through human love, however crude in expression, that light comes to the soul; or love bestowed on

---

flowers, perhaps, or on animals, or given to some person. *Love* is helping the inner light to grow; and the right reaction of the soul to bitter circumstances causes that light to become brighter too.

Thus the soul of man journeys onward, but not by a pitiless road. The soul may weary of its journey on earth, but the love of God mercifully blinds that soul so that it knows neither past nor future, but lives only in the present; and there are many beauties along the way, and recompense and satisfaction can come in countless forms. Visualise the man, staff in hand, walking this dusty, weary path, growing weary at eventide (or at the death of the physical body) and lying down to rest; and in the morning he awakens feeling like a man reborn. He *is* reborn, renewed and refreshed in those higher worlds; and so he starts off again for the next day's journey. Along the path he finds fruits growing which satisfy his hunger. He finds streams of crystal water to satisfy his soul's thirst. God is ever watchful and mindful of His children's needs.

As the man journeys, in due time and order he catches a glimpse in the distance of a cross raised against the sky. Humanity, the

---

earthly mind, has this picture presented to it as symbolic of the sacrifice of Jesus, but this is not all. The cross is an age-old symbol which all see at a certain stage of spiritual evolution; it is a symbol found through all races, all civilisations – an outward symbol of an inward experience, the experience of surrender, of complete self-giving. The neophyte, when first the bandage is taken from his eyes, beholds the light, and behind and in the light the cross of self-surrender. This is the first major initiation.

The cross is a symbol of life, but of life gained through death – death, not of the physical body, but of the dense lower self. The cross symbolises the surrender of the lower nature, the relinquishing of personal desire, the complete surrender to the will of God and the response to the inspiration of love and brotherhood.

This is not nearly so easy as it sounds, and if our words seem simple to you, let us again remind you that just as technical knowledge does not necessarily make a musician, neither does an accumulation of spiritual facts and knowledge make a saint. You may possess all knowledge, and still fail to find the key into the kingdom. The key

---

which will unlock the mysteries is found through the simple experiences of human life. These give the very gold of which the key is fashioned.

One of the primary lessons on the path is that of discrimination – discrimination between the false and the true; discrimination between the real and the unreal, between right and wrong; discrimination too between the promptings of your own higher or lower self. No one can teach us; no one can give us this divine attribute of discrimination. It is gained through experience and meditation.

Discrimination and discernment means getting your values right, and learning to look first at the spiritual aspect of every situation. If you have a problem, never try to answer that problem by the material standard only but look at it squarely and ask: 'What is the spiritual meaning of this?'. Always accept the spiritual value. Pray for true vision, and remember too that in helping others, as you all long to do, you help your brother to bear his burden, you stand by him as he crosses his bridge, but you do not try to take his karma from him, for his karma may help him to grow nearer to God.

———

Nor do you indulge him in things which are going to satisfy him only for the moment.

At the same time you have to learn not to sit in judgment on another. You cannot judge, for you do not know the past history of another, you do not know the karma which makes him act as he does, you cannot see that he may be an instrument of the great Lords of Karma. Man has not quite the degree of freewill in one life that you sometimes ascribe to him. The soul is placed in certain conditions in its physical life with circumstances arising continually which will give opportunities to serve the great law. Freewill lies in the soul's response; in its loving acceptance of the conditions it has been given, and in doing its best. That soul may – and invariably does – fail sometimes, indeed many times. No schoolboy can get through all his lessons perfectly, some are bound to be indifferently executed. So it is with human life. The elder brethren watch the struggles of those on earth with love and compassion. They do not say, 'That man is wrong!', and lash out with a harsh whip of judgment; but rather say, 'Dear brother, dear sister, you have done your best; we are sorry that you have to suffer'. The brother

———

or sister is enfolded in compassion and understanding of all the conditions and circumstances which have caused them to act as they have.

This is why we say to you, as we have done so many times before – *judge not.* We dare not judge, knowing that the one whom we may be tempted to judge is merely an instrument of the divine law. It is difficult for you to understand this. But part of the lesson of discrimination is to learn to discriminate between the laws of man and the laws of God, between the inner and the outer life. We have to learn to view every problem in the light of spiritual law, and in the light of love. Let us pray for ever greater understanding of God's law, and of God's love.

The soul who would receive the cross of light, who would bear that cross within his heart, must have learnt the lesson of discrimination and of complete surrender of the lower self to the divine; and when it comes to putting it into action in everyday life, this is one of the hardest lessons that man has to learn.

After the cross of light comes the quickening of the heart of love. From out of

---

the ashes of the lower nature arises the golden heart of pure love. Not a love which seeks its own; but a love which gives universally to life. This is the next step on the path.

In closing we would make this clear. The quality of soul-consciousness developing as the result of human experience is not gained in one brief incarnation; nor is a series of incarnations spent on one lesson alone. Usually many lessons, many desired attributes are being acquired during an incarnation. So we do not say that the soul passes one initiation after so many incarnations, and the next initiation after so many more. It is more likely that there is an all-round development, that many lessons are being learnt in many incarnations, which culminate in a series of initiations in one life. Or it may be that an initiation is taken in one distant life-period, and then a whole sequence of lives pass, while the soul acquires or absorbs many necessary qualities before the next initiation can take place.

Think of spiritual evolution as being a most perfect procedure . . . all the pieces and broken fragments of life are used, and brought together in an indescribably lovely

---

way, to perfect the pattern of man's life on earth.

And to our Father–Mother God we render all homage and worship; our hearts are full of thankfulness for the vision into the Golden World, and for the opportunities for service to God and man. The peace and love of the Great White Spirit is with us always.

Amen.

———

❦

———

3

THE PATH III

Almighty and Eternal Spirit of Wisdom, Love and Power, we aspire to Thee; we pray that we may be strengthened and helped on the path which leads to Thee. May the blessing of the holy angels be upon this gathering, and may each heart be touched by the love of Christ.

Amen.

THESE WORDS are so simple: 'May each heart be touched by the love of Christ'. Many times we have all heard similar words, and yet we forget them in the heat and stress of the outer life, especially when we are troubled with anxieties and fears and tribulation. If only we could bring our minds back to this simple truth, we should find all anger consumed, all fears dispelled, all weariness pass from us, with the very thought, or the realisation within our breast, that Christ's love is touching our hearts. His touch puts everything right. When we have experienced for ourselves the healing and comforting power of love, we know then the power of love to help another soul.

Before we speak to you about the heart of love, we would say again that the vision of the Christ light in the heavens, which comes as a result of the experience we have likened to crucifixion, is an important step on this path of spiritual growth. The lower self shrinks from this sacrifice; men and women prefer to keep themselves wrapped up in the clothing of materialism, and will not admit the existence of a spiritual life. They intuitively know that as soon as they admit the life of the spirit, which is the eternal life, then they must alter all their values, their moral standard, their whole attitude of mind towards life.

This is one reason why man refuses to listen to spiritual teaching. But we must also remember that another reason may make him reject the spiritual path. There are two types of materialist: those who, young in soul, are unawakened to the inner light; and those who *know*, deep within, but who feel urged to pursue a path on the outer plane because of a particular service they can render. It is impossible to judge from the outer aspect what is the motive, what lies behind another's actions.

It may be necessary for a soul to come back in a certain incarnation with other qualities of character more prominent, because he may have service to give at a more material level. If his service to humanity lies perhaps in the commercial world, it will be necessary for commercial instincts and gifts to have full play. The light from heaven would rather dazzle and divert him from his course. So the light is mercifully veiled for the time being. This will reveal how impossible it is for anyone to judge another soul.

This cross of sacrifice, or renunciation of desire of body, mind and, we are going to add, of spirit, we all, in due time, gladly welcome. We add 'of the spirit' because this path is like a razor's edge, its temptations are so subtle. Only by keeping the purpose pure and the Christ light burning steadily can we keep our feet on the path. Temptations which arise from the lower self crop up all the way. Even at the top of the ladder we may make a false step and fall, and then have to mount the steps once again.

———

Do not let this discourage you; bear in mind the reality of the inner light, and however much you are tempted by your own weakness and failure, keep on, keep on . . . keep on keeping on. Press forward. Do not give up the endeavour, for that is weak and futile, and will not help you. You cannot return to the place of blindness on the material plane; your eyes once having been opened, there is only one way for you, and that is forward. But beware of the temptation of selfish ambition urging you onward and upward on the spiritual path only because of the glories you will attain. This will not do.

Now, certain planetary influences demand renunciation. They give on the one hand, and they take on the other. Such influences take from you, and you have no choice in the matter. But although these influences rob you on the outer plane of possessions and conditions which you like and which you feel are good for you, remember always, we beg you, that God never takes without giving, and what is taken with one hand is given, in a different way, with the other. This is God's bounty, God's mercy and God's love.

———

So the candidate who treads the path leading to the portals of initiation must be prepared to welcome the cross of renunciation, or crucifixion. The soul growing strong, the soul in whom the flame begins to burn brightly, will face all renunciation philosophically, tranquilly, joyously. For that wise soul will *know* that that which is lost has served its purpose, its usefulness; and something better now awaits it. Whether on the spiritual or the material plane it does not know, but certainly something better awaits it. We must learn to face the cross with tranquillity, knowing that out of the ashes of the past is born a new life.

Pain and suffering so often come because a soul will cling to a condition which obviously must be withdrawn. But having learnt this lesson, having been willing to renounce, we receive fresh opportunities and greater blessings. We might even say that the Master's hand is laid upon the head of the pupil with, 'Well done, little brother . . .'

You ask, 'How can a soul renounce the world and human relationships when both are necessary to life?'. Brother, sister, son, daughter, father and mother – if these relationships were not necessary God would not have created them. Therefore we say human relationships are necessary, material life is necessary. They are serving a divine purpose. They are teaching and giving you experience through human emotion. But – and this is the crucial point – you must not be enslaved by the personality, by personal relationships, or by possessions and position or desire for these earthly things. Renunciation does not mean withdrawing from the world; for a man may renounce everything and still live in the world and retain his human relationships, but *within* that man or woman will be free, because deep within the heart there remains desire for nothing but to know more of the Great White Light, to grow nearer to the Great White Light and become reunited with this divine fire and light. Renunciation means putting the outer, the material and personal things of life in their right perspective. They have their uses: use them; but do not allow them to enslave you.

'I am willing, O Father–Mother God, to follow Thy light and will at all times. Use me as Thou wilt. I do not desire anything for myself; nothing that the earthly life can give me has any power over me. I only desire Thy will, to be a form of expression of Thy Son. I would be a rose growing in Thy garden radiating the sweet perfume of Thy love. I would grow, unnoticed, unrecognised by the passers-by. I would be content to be a rose in Thy garden.'

This is renunciation of all the lower self, the desires and ambitions of the world. You can live in the world but not be of the world. There is no self-assertiveness in the one who has renounced, only meekness and self-abnegation. But there is no weakness, my brethren, no weakness, but a great courage and dynamic strength, used in the service of God.

*

We look forward, then, to the next step, symbolised by the flaming heart of love, the heart afire with the love of Christ. When you sit in meditation you will gradually learn to be conscious of the heart as a light sending forth its rays. The heart centre is like the sun; it is indeed the sun of *your* solar system. The humanity of the future will learn to think with the heart. In the present day people think with the mind of the head, which has developed to such an extent that it almost extinguishes the light in the heart.

But men and women in the New Age will think from the mind of God which dwells in the heart. The more you respond to promptings of the heart in your human relationships, the more surely will you be treading the path of spiritual unfoldment. The mind of the future will function in the heart. Already it begins in those men and women who respond to intuition, who can so rule the mind in the head that it remains quiescent when so commanded. You also will find that in any perplexity, if you will learn to be still and let the heart speak, you will receive the direction you need. But it will come in the form of a *feeling*, an intuition. As your heart centre begins to open and develop, so you will begin to recognise the true guidance of the mind in your heart and respond to it.

One of the secrets held by an ancient brotherhood was the whereabouts of a key which would unlock the kingdom of God. 'Where hangs the key?' was the question; and the answer came, 'The key lies in the heart'.

On this path of love there are still many snares and delusions. So often sentiment is confused with love. Sentiment has its place, but sentiment is not love. Misplaced love – or sentiment – can blind a man to his real service to his brother; it will cause him to give foolishly, to indulge not only his brother, but also himself, indirectly. We see the illustration of the devoted mother, who gives the child everything it demands, thinking this to be love. What is the result? Far from giving her child opportunities to be happy, and to grow, the mother is robbing it of every chance of self-expression and development. The wise mother withholds lavish expenditure. This does not mean that she is cold and indifferent; but rather that her love is so great that she sees clearly the child's need for experience, that it must learn to make its own decisions. Comfort and console your brother, your child, yes; but help him to be strong, help him to make his own decisions, to gain his own experience. Too many sweets can make a child sick. If you indulge your brother and give him all he wants, thinking this is love, you are likely to give the equivalent of a bilious attack, to do more harm than good. And then, if you are wise, you will say: 'I have done enough mischief; I will no longer heap sweetmeats on the one I love. When I see him needing understanding and help, I will give him of my wisest and my best'.

The best help you can give to your brother is to be loving, understanding, sympathetic; sympathise with his aims and aspirations, and if he wants to take a certain path, do not say, 'I should not do this', but rather, 'If you feel that is the path, anything I can do to help I will do. I am with you all the way, my brother, in sympathy, in love. But you must work out your own salvation; I cannot do it for you'. Have we made it simple enough for you to understand the subtlety of this lesson of love?

When you learn to love, wisdom grows within you. We always couple wisdom and love, because true love begets wisdom. You cannot separate wisdom from love. To love truly is to put the need of your brother before your own; and to see clearly what is his greatest, his real need. You want to see him growing in spirit, in character, in strength of purpose. And to this end you give him your all.

May we indicate a trifling and a simple way of love? You may be very busy, full of your own affairs, with so much to do that you do not know how you will get through everything. Someone comes along who is obviously in need, who is poor – poor in love, poor in health. The temptation may be, because you are so busy, to push him on one side, not to bother with him. But love says: 'Other things can wait. This is my brother; his troubles are as real to me as my own'.

But do not let that brother *waste* your time. Gently lead him to unburden his heart to you; listen, and use your very best endeavours to see truth for him, and to say the kind, gentle, constructive things, which may bring the turning point in his life. Never be too busy to listen to a brother in need, to help him practically if need be. But at the same time be guided by wisdom, not overwhelmed by sentiment. So simple! Oh so simple, and it may not seem very important to you. But it is these little things which help to bring us close to the heart of universal love.

He who would love must be very careful not to hurt another by a careless word. Speak gently, thoughtfully. A slash with a sword can be painful. The pupil of the Master of love does not hurt another in any way, and this kindness and harmlessness embraces all life. Do your best to refrain

———

from hurting any form of life. This is love. There is so much cruelty in life. There is wanton cruelty, arising from selfishness, greed and violent emotion – and there is also cruelty arising from ignorance and thought-lessness.

To use a simple illustration. You have an animal friend, say a dog. If you love your friend you don't just caress and make a fuss of it (or indulge it!), but you understand its real need, and care for it. To love your little friend is to look after its needs. So also with flowers – another little thing: the nature kingdom is brought under the care of man, man takes upon himself to grow flowers, or to cut flowers, to use them to decorate his home. These flowers are sensitive; they have life-force in them and need your love. They call for loving attention; they want feeling from you. One who is on the path will love the animal and the plant, realising that these are forms of life, part of God even as he. He will respect the animal and nature king-doms, as he will respect his human brothers and love them.

You will say, 'How can we respect them when they do things which outrage all the laws of life?'. Respect that which you know dwells within your brother– the light of God, striving for growth and expression. Children draw pictures, and the results of their efforts are not always beautiful, but they are doing their best. Our brother may be drawing, or showing, a picture to the world which is unattractive; but it is a form of expression and growth; and, in a way we do not always appreciate, a form of service. It is difficult for you to understand that so-called evil and ugliness can be a form of service. But it is so. The attitude of one who loves is to endeavour to recognise always the *good* being contributed to life.

We have given you some homely similes; we have been simple perhaps in trying to show you what it means to love, but all these qualifications are necessary before the greater initiations are possible. Yet it is not enough that we renounce, and that we learn to love in a simple, human way. We must also become conscious of an inner development, the opening of the windows of the soul, those centres or vortices of psychic energy known in the East as chakras, which are situated at certain points along the spine, linked with the ductless glands and main nerve ganglions. Some will tell us that the qualifications of which we have been speaking are not necessary for the development of the inner faculties. But the only safe way as far as we ourselves can see is the way of self-discipline on the outer plane, together with the inner development of psychic and spiritual faculties.

We are sorry to have to leave you, but we do enfold you in love; every one of you we hold close to a big heart which loves you. White Eagle does not speak of himself, but of the greater heart behind. This great love is enfolding you, and so long as you are willing to be enfolded in this heart of love, it will hold you and give you sweetness and comfort and strength; it will give you nobility of character, it will give you inspiration to go on bravely on your allotted path; it will give you companionship, it will give you love and joy indescribable; and will in time reveal to you the glory of God's life.

We thank Thee, Father–Mother God.

We are bathed in the light. We bow our heads in reverence. We thank the Supreme One for our life, for all joy of growth and service. We know no other God but the God of love. We acknowledge also all wise brethren who have served mankind

---

since the foundation of the world; and above all, we bless God for the revelation of His spirit in the Son, Christ the Lord.

We call upon Him, in the name of the Father, so that He may use us, His younger brethren, in the service of creation.

Amen.

4

THE PATH IV

Let us with one accord, with simplicity of mind and heart, approach the throne of the Most High, All Good, our Father–Mother God. We pray that we may understand how to serve God and our brother man. We pray that our vision may be clear, our purpose steadfast and true, our love compassionate and gentle. May all become aware of the great brotherhood of love, the brothers in the light who love and serve mankind.

Amen.

BEFORE WE continue our theme, we would like to present to your imagination the picture of a perfect rose. Its petals are open to the sunlight; and the dew is upon those petals. Inhale if you can the fragrant perfume of this rose, and as you inhale you will feel the blessing and inspiration which comes from the substance of which that flower is created. . . .

We want you to understand that all the physical senses have their etheric counterpart. With the etheric counterpart of your sight, your hearing, your sense of smell, of touch and taste, you may become aware of beautiful forms which live for a time, indeed perhaps for eternity, on those higher planes.

The rose is a symbol of the love which we spoke of last time. It is frequently pictured as upon the cross – the rose of life, which will bloom at the heart of humanity's cross when humanity has completed its spiritual evolution and become regenerated, reborn, into the Christ-man. The rose, then, may symbolise man made perfect, the Christ-man.

Jesus Christ said to the rich man who had asked him what he should do to gain eternal life: *Sell that thou hast, and give to the poor.* The young man turned away sorrowfully, because he had great possessions. This is usually interpreted to mean material possessions – but the Master did not specify the kind of possessions to which he referred. Does not this really mean that man must be ready to give up all that he most truly prizes? All pride of possessions must go, whether these possessions be worldly goods, mental attainments, or spiritual jewels. St John

———

describes in the Book of Revelation how the twenty-four elders cast down their crowns before the throne of God. Every man must one day come to the point where he says, 'God, I cast my crown before thee, for it is of no use to adorn my head. All that I have and am I give back to Thee. My brothers need my service – this is all that concerns me now. I go, unadorned, to serve life'.

Pride of possession is a subtle temptation, which all face in many varied ways. We all cling to possessions in one form or another, but we have to arrive eventually at that point of spiritual growth where we know that all possessions, all gifts, all attainments, belong to God. Of ourselves we are nothing; we live and move and have our being only in the consciousness of our Father God.

In this realisation man is wealthy beyond all earthly dreams; in coming to the realisation of true wealth man becomes consciously part of the great universal power, which is his to use, not for himself, but for the good of the whole.

We have tried to make it clear that the goal of man's spiritual quest is the realisation of this God-consciousness. To achieve such a goal there must come this surrender of self, this 'selling all that thou hast' or this 'casting down the crown of glory before the throne of God'. Man can hold *nothing* to himself; it is against the great Law. But by truly giving himself, man becomes at one with God, the universal life-force. This truth should be applied to the smallest detail in the life of the aspirant.

Something is taking place in the aspirant when he applies the simple rules of renunciation, compassion, wisdom, love and service to his daily life. Many methods were and are used in the East, and to some degree in the West, to open up the centres of power, or the windows of the soul in the subtler bodies of man. Such methods certainly can release power, and bring a certain degree of illumination. But with the close application of the rules of the spiritual path to everyday life, these windows of the soul cannot help but be cleansed, and opened naturally to the heavenly life. With the practice of true brotherhood, for instance, the heart centre becomes stimulated; the throat centre begins to expand and radiate light, and the head centre begins gently to stir and open and become an instrument of divine intelligence. The centres of the lower triangle of the body also begin to take more beautiful form, coming under the control and dominion of the higher triangle . . . of wisdom, love and power from the God-man, the Christ-man.

By following the mystical path of meditation, development and growth through daily life, these windows of the soul will open naturally and sweetly. This is not forced growth; on the path of development there are great temptations and dangers, and with *forced growth* great care is needed. Forced growth can be delicate, and the flower so produced may wither, and the plant from which it sprang may have to be carefully tended before it regains its life and vigour. But the plant which grows under natural conditions, which has weathered the storm, the wind and the rains, has a good chance of producing strong, fragrant flowers, and good fruit.

Thus there are two paths open before the soul: the way of love, the mystical way; and the way of the more forced, occult growth. Some can stand the second way, and come through fine and well trained. But it is a difficult path, beset with dangers. We do not say that the mystical path is not also difficult. In some ways it can be a heart-breaking path. We suggest therefore that on this mystical path the great need is for dispassion. You become very sensitive; you feel acutely the effects of the words and actions of your fellows. These you must learn to take wisely and dispassionately. Having had the heart, the throat and the head centres stimulated to some degree, you become sensitive to the thoughts and words of others. It is therefore of the utmost importance that you develop inner strength and poise; you must learn to become dispassionate and turn your thoughts outward towards the well-being of others, instead of inwardly brooding on your own hurts, faults and failings. Many waste too much time in introspection . . . they wonder if this or that is right, if this or that is wrong; so eager and so anxious are they to progress. But this is a weakness which must be overcome. A few mistakes do not matter. It is what you are thinking, what you contribute in love, compassion and great-heartedness to humanity that is all-important.

Above all, do not turn inwards to brood on imagined wrongs. Know that all men are both pupils and teachers. You may be pupil to one man or woman; you may be teacher to

---

another. Do not be disconcerted or even affected by what goes on around you, but keep quietly on, knowing that all are striving (even as you are striving) to develop God-consciousness.

When you have learned to be dispassionate you will appear to the Watchers as a steady, sure instrument, which can be used by the Elder Brethren, the masters of the wisdom. If need arises, then you are ready; you stand forth as a server. Your light shines; you are seen from far distances, and will be used to do constructive work amongst men. How can you be used until this dispassion, this steadfastness has been attained? The Elder Brethren will not know what your reactions will be in certain circumstances. But when you have been tested, when you have come through your tests strong and robust, you can then be depended on by the Elder Brethren to do whatever piece of work is entrusted to you – you will do it as a well-trained soldier obeying the commands of his superior officer.

You must be prepared. Your superior officer issues his commands through the still small voice. And the man or woman who has learned to respond will hear the voice above

---

all the noise and clamour of the world. The cultivation of dispassion, quiet stillness in the breast, will enable the aspirant to hear clearly the voice of the Master whose commands he awaits.

You will say: 'How am I to be sure?'. This is always the question – 'Is this voice *really* the voice of the Master?'. Jesus said *By their fruits ye shall know them.* If a voice tells you to do certain things which your conscience knows to be good, loving, kind and wise, then the voice is true. But if that voice tantalises, worries, confuses, it is not coming from the true source, and you can disregard it. The Master's is a voice of love, justice, goodness and wisdom, and is without criticism or condemnation.

We say again that he who would be worthy of initiation into the temple of the mysteries must learn to be unaffected, undisturbed by those things which usually cause the less understanding, or the younger brother, to become fearful, angry or confused – states of mind which must cut him off from the blessings of God which indeed are his birthright. Man is forfeiting his birthright when he succumbs to violent passion.

At the beginning of our talk we presented

---

for your meditation the picture of the rose. Now as we close we ask you to visualise the form of the water-lily. Let us see this pure white flower resting on the surface of the still water, its roots reaching down into the mud beneath. Let us see in this symbol a picture of the soul which has become at peace, which is stilled, untouched by the storms and passions of life, the soul which has learned the lessons of dispassion.

This symbol, as we gaze on it, should bring to our waiting hearts the state of dispassion which we seek. It is a symbol of renunciation, of surrender. It tells the Silent Watchers when the soul is ready and waiting to be guided towards the gates of heaven . . .

Great Spirit of love, we only pray to become more aware of Thy glory; that our light may grow more bright, more steady, so that others travelling along life's journey may see the light, and be welcomed to the simple home of love which we would build for all the wayfarers on the path of life.

Amen.

⊙✛⊚

❧

5

THE PATH V

HAVING passed through the lessons of renunciation and dispassion, and having learnt something of how to love, the soul is ready to advance towards the great portal of initiation. We would classify initiations as of two types: the first are minor; the second, major initiations. The former are continually being experienced in human life, and may pass without recognition of their true value to the candidate. The major initiations are definite spiritual experiences, which cannot be gone through without the candidate being aware. Every soul initiated into the heavenly wisdom passes through initiation in full consciousness of the experience, although the absorption of this may take some time. Minor initiations are what all persons experience during their many incarnations, experiences which deeply affect the

---

soul, opening up the understanding of neo-phytes to the true values of life and of their right relationships with their fellows.

Great upheavals in the human life, the changes and decisions which come in the course of that life, can be regarded as minor initiations. The soul learns through sorrow and joy alike, and all these experiences should bring to that soul an ever-greater wisdom and understanding of its fellows and of itself. These lesser initiations are con-tinually taking place throughout an incarna-tion. But if the lesson has been unregistered, if the pupil has failed to learn a lesson in one incarnation, the soul will be confronted with the same lesson, again and again in subse-quent lives, until the lesson is learnt. It is well that we should be alert to the lessons with which the Great Lords of Karma are pre-senting us, and be thankful for each lesson as it comes, for thus we proceed along the path of spiritual evolution on our return journey to our Father–Mother God.

Major initiations are experienced by those who have travelled along the pro-bationary path, and cause a stimulation of the upper triangle of the heart, throat and head centres. However we should not separate these three points from the lower triangle, the solar plexus, sacrum and root centre, in their relationship to major initiations; all these points of light in man may gradually grow into life and power on the journey along the path.

We would not divide major initiations into watertight compartments, and say that at the first initiation such and such a thing takes place, and in the second initiation something else, and so on. We would rather say that there is a general stimulation of the *goodness* in the individual soul, a growing on many levels at the same time, rather than a separate stimulation of any one point.

In the beginning, when the soul is a babe starting out upon this long path of growth and development of the spiritual powers with which he is endowed, he is to be seen from a spiritual aspect, as a tiny flame, a 'little light'. (For those who bear memories of the Egyptian rites, 'little light' should strike a chord of memory.) Man came from God, and to God he returns. The spirit of man is as a 'little light', a little spark of life which came from the sun, not the sun you see in your sky, but the eternal universal sun, the sun behind the sun. We are all as tiny flames,

———

breathed forth from that sun, and during the process of evolution this 'little light' grows, and becomes, at length, a blazing sun–star, a Christ.

Thus as the soul proceeds along the path, the light grows brighter; but not until it has travelled a long, long journey does this light within start to spread and radiate outside the form enclosing it. Picture a dark room, with a night-light burning in it. Such is the appearance of the one in whom the light has not yet grown bright and strong. Those who watch over mankind, looking for those likely to be of service, the Silent Watchers of humanity, can see immediately when the light is strong enough to lead, to guide others, and when that light can be used, can be stimulated and fanned into a fire. By the light within is man known to his teacher and his master.

Will you, on the other hand, imagine a house illumined throughout, with every window open, and the light streaming forth across the quiet countryside; or maybe, across the great city within which it is placed? Compare the two: the first, the little chamber with the tiny light, barely visible; and on the other hand the house which is a blaze of light and warmth, a beacon shining across the countryside, or casting a great light in the city. This is the huge difference between a young soul whose light is still hidden, and the elder soul, casting the rays of spiritual light far and wide.

To God we return! . . . God is the light within: we are returning to God, grown in God's likeness, sons and daughters of God, of the light. Each 'window' in the house is one of the sacred chakras, which gradually become stimulated and alight through many initiations of minor degree, and are brought at last to full power and full radiance by the major initiations, by spiritual experience, spiritual illumination.

*

Many of our friends on earth, particularly those who have 'seen the light', are eagerhearted, full of enthusiasm: so anxious to progress, they want to 'rush the gates of heaven'. But the over-hasty come up against an instrument, invisible, but sharp, which causes the eager heart to pause. There can be no rushing forward on the path of spiritual enlightenment. The lessons, which affect every plane of man's being, must be thoroughly learnt. These lessons can be interpreted in astrological terms as those of the earth, air, fire and water elements. You cannot hope to conquer, to become master in any one of these elements in one brief incarnation, and so the soul puts forth a fresh feeler in each incarnation, and according to its need the earth, the fire, the air, or the water aspect of life is emphasised that the soul may gain strength and experience through the lessons of that particular element.

In the physical body, time is your master, and often a difficult one; but time also is a great teacher, and maybe you are learning the wisdom of Father Time even now. Saturn, sometimes portrayed as Father Time, is strict with his pupils, and permits no hurried lessons, no hasty sums or superficial essays. He insists on due time being given to every lesson. Those who would hurry through 'unpleasant' lessons should remember this venerable, gracious and wise teacher.

When initiation comes it means not only a great expansion of consciousness, but also it brings increased power, and power can be destructive. Misuse of power can throw a soul right back on the path. The Bible tells of Lucifer, who, having gained great power, became a light in heaven, but was cast forth because of this misuse of power. We recognise there can be more than one interpretation of Lucifer's fall, but we use this story to illustrate the possibilities of the soul which, attaining power without the corresponding wisdom and love, becomes liable to a great fall.

Thus we see the wisdom of God, for if a soul *does* rush forward, it is bound to come up against that sharp instrument and be driven back. It is far better to proceed simply and slowly and naturally. Never try to hurry, or force, spiritual advancement.

On the path of spiritual unfoldment, we must recognise three distinct paths running parallel, yet which also overlap each other. First comes the training and preparation of the physical body; next, the training and preparation of the soul; and lastly, the training and the discipline and awakening of the spirit. Once arrived at that point on the path where initiation begins, we shall find tests in preparation for this initiation on each one of these planes – body, soul and spirit. We always advise moderation, and gentle development, but there are certain truths necessary for us to recognise in our training for initiation.

On the soul vibration we meet with perhaps the first and greatest test – that of *dispassion*. The soul is by nature emotional, and easily becomes indignant, upset, and hurt by trifling things. To become dispassionate, we think, is one of the most important lessons; a statement which bears repetition. The soul must learn to keep its equilibrium and not get unduly upset. Do not fly into a rage because something does not please you, or because someone has hurt you; do not give way to depression, but endeavour to attain and maintain an even and still vibration.

Many other subtle lessons come to test and try would-be aspirants on the path. We are tested for fear. We are also tested for discrimination, and so many of us fall on that stile. We cannot discriminate between the false and the true. We cannot discriminate between good and evil. We do not even understand what good and evil are. But these lessons have to be learned. If you come up against a certain experience which you would do anything to escape from or alter; and if the lesson proves very hard to bear, then go through with a patient and steady spirit, knowing that through the experience, wisdom is growing in your heart, and also that you are clearing the way for further growth, paying off a past debt. And more than this, you are being given an opportunity to learn the lesson of dispassion. However difficult that human experience may prove, it will be worthwhile.

One other point of the utmost importance on the spiritual path, is that of spiritual arrogance. How often did the Master Jesus stress that lesson throughout His ministry, again and again laying bare the hypocrisy of the Pharisee. This same lesson is one bound to confront every soul, and it comes in many subtle forms. The soul setting forth on the spiritual path can become inflated with its own spiritual progress and power. Having started out with a pure desire to serve humanity, after advancing to a certain extent along the path, he begins to feel that he is a fine fellow, and doing a magnificent work. Mind you, this kind of thing is helped on by others, who pour adulation upon him and say 'how wonderful you are!'. The recipient of unwise praise begins to think 'Yes, I do sacrifice a lot . . .' and so forth. Then comes the test; that soul has to face an unexpected test of its spiritual fealty and truth, and its spiritual humility.

Only if the soul has striven with all its might to follow in the footsteps of Christ; only if the spirit of that man or woman has endeavoured truly to reflect the gentle humility of the Christ; only then can it never lose itself in self-glorification, for it knows that it is neither great nor wonderful, that of itself it could not heal, teach, nor give comfort; it knows that any good flowing through it is of Christ, is of God. The test, dear ones, is that of the Christ Spirit; and if you can truly feel that the gentle humble spirit of the Son of God is walking by your side, your hand in His, you cannot fail.

In this connection we would emphasise the value of the training on the three planes, through meditation. Do not overdo, but do not neglect the daily meditation. Try to set aside a time, even if only five minutes in the morning and at night, for this purpose. Try never to fail in this daily contact with the eternal Source of light and truth, because this daily meditation will help you at three levels; it will train the *body* in self-control, making it do that which your spirit desires

_____

rather than letting it have its own way; it will train and control the *mind*, and it will help to bring body, mind and emotions under the directing power of the spirit.

As we have already said, the major initiations applying to humanity come under four elements – earth, air, fire and water. This is one explanation (though not the only one) of the ancient symbol of the cross within the circle. The peoples of the lost continents held this symbol in great reverence, for they respected and worshipped the angels of the four elements it represents.

In taking these initiations the soul of man must pass every test of the fire, the earth, the air and the water elements. The soul must be in communion, in brotherhood, with all life-forms on these rays – all the elementals and nature spirits, the angels and gods controlling these four elements. Man, while on earth, starts in a humble way to learn to control these elements within his own character, within his own life, and to gain mastery over them. And as he does this he wins the co-operation of the nature spirits, learning to walk in harmony with them. If you will study the miracles and parables of Jesus, you will see demonstrated his mastery over and co-operation with the spirits of these elements. The elder brother does not pit himself against them, but seeks their co-operation through love and wisdom, through brotherhood, and through his mastery of the elements in himself.

The lesson of the air element is that of brotherhood. People learning this lesson find that it is not enough to live to themselves, but that their humanity must expand to touch all lives. They must work in harmony with all life: not only human life but, beyond this, with the spirits of the air, the sylphs and the great angels of air, who control the air-currents, the storms and the winds, and who work sometimes in collaboration with the undines and the great spirits of the water. Souls learning the lesson of the air element have also to learn to control that powerful human mind, breaking down its arrogance, bringing it under the control of the spirit, teaching it humility. The truly great and wise man is tolerant, simple and humble.

The lesson of the fire element is that of love. Love is the magic fire, the great life-force, and within this element comes magic. (We will not differentiate between black and

---

white magic, because both are the same, the difference being in the way the magical power is used.) Love itself is magical, even in its simplest human form. The soul that truly loves radiates a certain magnetism through its love. Men say, 'There is something about So-and-So, I am drawn to him'. That magical force is really the love, the fire element. Those learning the lesson of the fire element are learning to use the white magical power of love.

Love is a magical principle, a worker of miracles. Those under this fiery influence must endeavour to use this magical principle to give light and comfort and joy to their brothers and sisters on earth. They will also have 'green fingers' for growing things, and fire will respond to them quickly, too.

Love is a creative force. Yet it has such power that it can also be destructive if it is not allied to wisdom. Love and wisdom must go hand in hand, for ungoverned emotion (which is not real love) can be harmful and destructive. Souls with a strong element of fire must remember that all the fire spirits, from the salamander to the great spirits of the fire, of the Sun, all come within their orbit. The salamanders, the little fire people,

57

will work for you, and help you to make a fire quickly; but if you offend them they may cause you to burn your fingers, and if you offend gravely they may burn something more valuable than fingers!

Water teaches the lesson of peace. A beautiful element, a beautiful influence! (Do not however think that any one element is *better* than another. Remember the cross within the circle; all elements have an exactly equal place in the great scheme of man's evolution, as well as in the great scheme of creation.)

The influence of water mainly affects the soul, the astral plane, the psyche and psychic things, and the candidate working with the water element has to learn to control astral forms, astral elements, the emotions and desires of the astral body. These desires can be troublesome indeed, and the emotional and desire body will make many claims upon you. You have to learn to control this element *within yourself* before you can advance towards the next step, and control astral forces and astral life.

Finally, the lesson of the earth element is that of service and sacrifice. He who is treading the path towards the earth initiation is learning to bring the light, the divine magic, right through from the spiritual heights into perfect action and expression on earth. The soul comes to know that ultimately all that has been learned of spiritual truth, all that has been gained, must be surrendered, given back in loving humble service on earth. The keynote of the element is humility.

The soul learning the lesson of the earth element is learning to work with exactness and precision to perfect the rough ashlar of his being.

To attain mastership, the spirit of the man must gain mastery over all the lower planes of life. It must be master of his physical, emotional and mental bodies. It must attain command over the lower vehicles, as a captain commands his ship. When a measure of control has been earned, when the earthly tests have been safely passed, the time comes for that man to be summoned into the great Hall of Initiation (and no-one is overlooked when ready for initiation into the knowledge of the Great Light). The soul is led by the guide through many intricate ways, many dark passages — which is what you are now going through in your earth life, when you do not know whither your road leads, nor when you will turn the corner, nor what you will find when you round it. Your human life is really like a passage through which the being, man, is being led by the guide, through many incarnations, until at long last he comes into a gracious and beautiful place, and is led up to the altar of light, so brilliant that the eyes must be veiled. But at the end of the great ceremony the eyes open to behold the blazing star, the star of six outer points but with one central point, making seven in all. This seven-pointed star corresponds to the seven great rays of life, the seven rays which come from the seven angels round the throne of God. Through his long, long journey man has also been learning, training, gaining power in order to send forth the light from every one of the seven sacred centres in his own body, and to draw on the seven sacred planetary forces which work through the signs of the zodiac. Perfected man not only *sees* that blazing star at his initiation, but realises in a moment of supreme illumination that he is himself that Star.

And unto the Great White Spirit we turn our faces, and we receive into our souls His love, His wisdom and His power . . . and we bless and thank Him. May we become ever more worthy to walk in His light.

Amen.

❧

END OF THE FIRST PART

6

THE SECOND COMING

Great White Spirit, we bow in prayer before Thy glory. May thy blessing be upon the work of the illumination of mankind. May all hearts be drawn together in the spirit of love. May they receive illumination of their hearts and minds and become aware of the multitude of spiritual beings, angelic and human, with whom they live, although they know it not, and with the gracious presence of our Lord and King, the Son Christ.

Amen.

YOU HAVE BEEN told many times of the great development which is coming on the earth, when life will be harmonious and beautiful, and when men and women will live together in the brotherhood of the spirit. But sometimes you are discouraged by what you see; you look upon the sufferings of humanity and feel indeed you are gazing upon another crucifixion of Christ. You must not be cast down, dear brethren, but look up, and endeavour to see the vast company of shining spirits, men and angels, whose light is slowly penetrating the mists surrounding the earth. Those unhappy conditions which distress you so much will pass. Remember they are working out a purpose in matter; and the day will come when you will be filled with joy and thanksgiving at the outworking of the divine plan.

For you have either to accept the omnipotence and omniscience of the Great Spirit, the great Intelligence which is guiding and directing human life, or to reject and deny it. Too much has happened in your own lives for you honestly to deny the supreme, loving, wise Intelligence which is guiding your destiny. Therefore you must give all to that wisdom and love and have no doubts. You say, 'We do not question God's love and wisdom, but only doubt *man's* wisdom, which seems on occasion to be non-existent'. Nevertheless, if you accept the omnipotence and omniscience of the divine Spirit you must recognise that God's plan for creation is also perfect, and that within all God's creatures lies the seed of a perfect blossom.

We must all work together, you in the

_____

body and we in the spirit, to bring to mankind the food for which it is starving. We must bring to man that which he needs for his sustenance and his growth. It is common in the world for you to criticise one another; it is easy to see the wrong that others do. But the Master Jesus would instead have you concentrate your attention on your own actions and thoughts, and gently advise you to look within before you blame others. Be strict with yourself, but sympathetic with others. This is not easy; but every thought and act of yours is either helping the rest of creation, or retarding its progress. You will exclaim 'Oh, but my trivial thoughts and acts are swallowed up in the whole and cannot have much, if any, effect upon life'. The ancient sages always taught their pupils that all depended upon individual thought and action, upon individual human effort; and that each individual soul was responsible for the progress or otherwise of life in matter.

In past ages, humanity has touched the depths and has been encased in matter as in an iron box. Now it is gradually being released. Remember, too, my brethren, that to many people the earthly mind is like an iron box which they cannot break. Man is gradually, slowly but surely, beginning to release himself from bondage. Man *must* release himself. The key to this release is the light that God has implanted in his heart.

You look forward to the Second Coming of Christ, for it is said so clearly that Christ will come again. You have heard us say on many occasions that this Second Coming will be in the heart of every man and woman. It will be the awakening of the light. When this light burns bright in the human soul, then will come about the purification of matter, of the physical body, the earth; the control of the emotional, the desire body; and, perhaps a greater task still, the control of the mental body. After that will come the birth of the divine, the Christ-man. The Moon represents the soul, the Sun represents the spirit. Before man can attain mastery over this earth there must come about the marriage or perfect union between the mental and the spiritual body. This is the difference between the man of earth and the man of heaven.

We have already spoken about the initiations of the elements: the initiation of water, which means the control of the emotional body, the purification of the emotional body;

---

and the air initiation, which is the control of, the purification of, the mental body, and the mastery of it; the initiation of fire – the fire element through which the soul learns how to use the white magic which is love; and the initiation of earth, which means the control of the body and also the crucifixion of the lower nature. An initiation, remember, is an unfoldment or expansion of understanding, an expansion of spiritual awareness; but this initiation does not necessarily come through some occult or religious ceremony. In your daily life there are many occasions when, for one reason or another, you experience an expansion of awareness. You may have some question which puzzles you, and to which you can find no answer; and perhaps, as you think about or meditate upon it, you may go into a bookshop or library and find yourself selecting a book at random; or perhaps a friend may chance to lend you a book, and as a result of reading this book, or perhaps even through a chance conversation, an idea will come to you in a flash. Where before you were puzzled, it will seem to you as though a great light suddenly floods your mind, and as a result of that light percolating your mind, a whole new vision will open before you. In other words, there has come an expansion of vision, of consciousness.

Yet again, an expansion of consciousness might be associated with some particular event of a material nature which may bring about a very big change in your life. You may experience intense joy or have to undergo deep sorrow, an experience which brings you a deeper and wider understanding of life. This is what we mean by an initiation brought about through daily life.

On the other hand, there are certain initiations we connect with spiritual work, certain ceremonies which can be undergone, initiation into a Masonic Lodge, for example, or an initiation into any Lodge associated with spiritual truth. Then again, something happens to your soul; your soul is played upon by certain spiritual powers and these powers help to quicken the spiritual life-forces in your soul body. This can again cause a flash of enlightenment, an expansion of consciousness.

Understand, however, that you yourselves must *work* in your everyday life; it is your reactions to physical matter and the conditions of life that really bring about attunement, achievement. It is no good listening to White Eagle, or to anyone else, unless you yourself work for self-mastery. The beginning of this work is your awareness of the still small voice within, of that gradually increasing light in you which causes you to react as a gentle brother to all the conditions and all the circumstances of life.

The way to open the vision and awaken the consciousness is through meditation. By meditation we mean a going *beneath* all thought to the level of spiritual life, and becoming aware of the light and the power which is within you which the ancient sages called the solar force. This solar force is sacred and must only be stimulated when the individual is earnestly seeking the truth and the life of Christ, and not for selfish motives or to satisfy curiosity. In the temples of the past, in the mystery schools, this knowledge was guarded most carefully. It is still withheld from the masses. But in the new Aquarian Age this knowledge, although still sacred and secret, is being given to true seekers, who are humble and pure in heart. The beginning of this stimulation lies in prayer and meditation, which, as we have already told you, means quiet, rhythmic breathing, a stilling of the outer mind, a going into the inner temple, and there seeking the Lord of the Light. This procedure affects the whole body.

In approaching the invisible worlds, man has to hold a pure love in his heart, first of all for his brother man, and then for all creation. He has to love the elementals, for they play a very big part in helping the adept or the master in his work for mankind. At present there is war between man and the elementals; as man advances, there must come peace, friendship, indeed almost marriage between the two. We do not mean marriage in the human sense, but in the heavenly. There must come this friendship, this harmony, between man and the elementals.

You have a demonstration of this vital truth in the miracles of the Master Jesus. We are particularly thinking of the miracle of Jesus walking upon the water, and of Jesus stilling the storm. This has more than one meaning, we admit, but for the present let us say that his walking on the water symbolises his complete control of the water element, the emotions – for the water element affects the emotions. He did not sink. His brothers, the water spirits, supported him, and he in turn

---

was able to support his disciple while he held fast to trust and faith in his Master. The same thing happened when he stilled the storm. The air spirits, the sylphs, came to his assistance, obeyed his command. In order to obtain true mastery over the elements of earth, air, fire and water, man must become like the Son of God, all love, all tenderness, and so filled with this solar power. He must win their respect and their love.

Remember that the purpose of your life is to grow, first of all in self-consciousness, then in group consciousness, a consciousness of the whole brotherhood of life. You have sometimes expressed in meditation the intense joy felt in the realisation of this spiritual brotherhood – which of course is the true spiritual communion, or development of the soul towards awareness of the needs of those around it. In the same degree as the individual progresses, so, collectively, the whole race approaches this point of brotherhood and awareness. Then, instead of perpetual warfare and strife, the brotherhood of angels and of men will have become a living reality.

Today such a statement seems incredible. Nevertheless we repeat that the next stage to self-consciousness is that state where man becomes aware of his true relationship to his brother man; then will come an expansion still further towards God-consciousness or cosmic consciousness; and then the next step is the solar consciousness, the consciousness of the Solar Logos. This is taking you a long way ahead. However, read our words and meditate on this truth, because this vision of the future life will make you feel that your present striving is worth all the suffering and the effort. Remember, if you are listening to the voice of the spirit, that you are pioneers working for the great day when cosmic and solar consciousness will be realised by all people. *Know* that the world is not going to remain in its present state of chaos.

We would take you into the glorious ceremony in the heavens of the manifestation of the Solar Logos, the Christ spirit, the Son of God.* You are apt to talk too glibly about the Son of God and the Christ. You accept the Christ as an ideal; some of you

*These words were spoken at the time of the Christ festival, at the full moon with the sun in the sign of Gemini.

———

recognise the Christ spirit as gentle and meek and loving, something that is wholly at one with something within yourself. You fail to understand the immense glory of that great Solar Logos, which is the life of all men and the life of this planet and solar systems. You do not understand, dear ones, that this outpouring of golden light comes down and can reach you, if you are sufficiently humble and simple and can open your heart to the blessing.

Remember that that solar force is within yourself in a lesser degree. It is within you, buried deeply, and lies there dormant. This is better so, until man rises of his own freewill to worship truth, to worship and adore the Son of God, profoundly, from the depths of his being. When the soul feels adoration and worship for the Solar Logos, the blazing Sun in the heavens, the only-begotten Son of the Father–Mother God, then that soul feels a stirring within, as the mother feels the quickening of her child. Then will come the rising of this solar force into your etheric body, your physical body, into all your bodies; and every centre will become alive and will open as a flower opens to the sunlight. Then you will progress from realisation of your brotherhood with your fellows to the realisation of your at-one-ment with the Christ, and a new consciousness of God will dawn in your heart.

A yogi is one who has attained God-consciousness, or conscious union with God, and it does not matter whether he wears a yellow, brown, black, white or red skin. You too can attain this degree of God-consciousness, union with God; and from this stage go forth into solar consciousness, which is a condition beyond your comprehension, but something that waits for you in the future.

Down the ages mystery schools have been formed to help the simple and earnest souls to understand the mysteries of life and 'death'. They taught both the lesser and the greater mysteries of life. To receive such knowledge the soul had to be pure and simple, because otherwise the knowledge of the mysteries might prove dangerous to it. Spiritual forces can be misused, with dire results. Thus it was never easy to enter a mystery school. Only after much testing and trial was the candidate admitted and taught how to stimulate this solar fire, this solar force, and use it for the glory of God and for the blessing and upliftment of men, not only by living the life but by doing the works of the Father–Mother in heaven.

There is a great deal to learn, my brethren. A world of unfolding beauty will open when you take the trouble to tread the path, proceeding by the way of meditation, prayer, devotion; not by ostracising yourself from ordinary life, but by living in the world as a son, a daughter of God. Meditation will take you right up through all the planes into the heavenly light, into that celestial world of the perfected sons and daughters of God. *Eye hath not seen nor ear heard, the things which God hath prepared for them that love Him.* This, my brothers, is the path which the Aquarian Age opens up, beauty and harmony and brotherhood from earth to heaven. Then Jacob's ladder will be raised upon the earth and every seeker whose vision is quickened will see the angels coming and going 'twixt earth and heaven'. You will learn for yourself that we speak the truth. We cannot give you proof, but the proof is waiting for you to find in your own evolution. Do not be content to listen to our words or to read the writings of the initiates and mystics and sages. *Seek truth for yourselves* and you will surely find the jewel, a treasure of great price.

———

God bless you. May you receive God's blessing – now.

Now let us all draw together as a one whole to thank the Great White Spirit for the revelation of the truth of the spiritual force which is now coming to mankind. Let us pray that we may have courage to stand for this truth and to impart it by life, by service to the spirit of our brother man. May we be caught up in the fire of divine love, the Christ spirit, and be held for ever in its heart.

Amion.

———

———

❦

7

MAN – HUMAN AND DIVINE

We bring you the love of the spirit company who are with us . . .

WE HAVE chosen to speak on the subject of man, human and divine. Perhaps some of you think that humanity does not appear to have a very great deal of the divine in it, but we in spirit look out upon the world and we see so much to love in mankind. Humanity at heart is very tender and it would be good if our brethren on earth would strive to recognise the divinity in their brother man. For man *is* divine. The elements of divinity are in the physical body as well as in the soul of man. Take the human form: when it stands upright with feet on the earth, head in the heavens, arms outstretched to serve, to give, to love, the symbol of the cross is made. The cube too is a symbol of man in incarnation –

---

the rough stone (in Masonic language, the rough ashlar) which has to be smoothed and perfected before it can be built into the temple. And when the cube is opened out we have again the form of the cross.

In ancient days the people took the human body as their symbol for the study of the universe. They were taught that in the physical body were to be found all the elements of the universe, that every part of the physical body – brain, throat, heart, circulatory system, generative system, hands, feet, fingers, toes, the whole of the body, had some connection with the stars and planets, and with the divine universe. Thus the men of antiquity were taught to study the human body to learn the secrets of the universe and of God. The words, 'Man, know thyself, and thou shalt know God and the universe' were emblazoned over the entrance to the temples of the past, and every candidate had to follow the path of self-knowledge, and to study the mysteries of the human body. Remember, therefore, to take care of the physical body, for it is the temple of God; the very essence of God is pulsating through your veins. The body is the clothing of the spirit; and the spirit, centred in the heart of man, permeates every physical atom.

You may have wondered why in certain pictures of the Master Jesus the heart is depicted with light streaming from it. This is because the heart centre is the home, the seat of the divine spark, the true self, the Christ self. The other two centres about which the priests of the ancient wisdom taught their students were the head centre (the brain, the intellect) and the creative centre, the generative centre. If man is ruled by the lower centres, he is a materialist – he lives for the pleasure of the body and this one life. If he is ruled by his head centre and is an intellectualist, he lives for the things of the mind. But if he is governed by his heart centre, the centre of wisdom and light, then he is an initiate. The centre of the heart, the centre of wisdom and love, should control and balance the other two. If you could see with clairvoyant vision the form of the true initiate of the ancient wisdom, you would see that it is like a cone of light. From the apex of that cone, the light streams down into the form of man, controlling the mind, the brain, and the lower centres of his being.

With each successive incarnation, fresh

opportunity is opened up before you to bring the divine light through into physical manifestation. Each one of you is a son or a daughter of God. Only a part of your true self manifests through your physical body; your higher self is withdrawn from physical matter but it is still connected with your personality. As you aspire to truth, to purity, to Christliness in the widest sense of the word, you are bringing that higher self, the divine self, through into full manifestation. The whole purpose of man's incarnation is that he may eventually manifest the divine life, the life of God, through physical matter. Man on earth must eventually show forth the glory of God.

It is a mistake to think that as soon as you leave your physical body you will be free to enter the heavens, or that you will automatically have all the spiritual attributes; for when you pass from your physical body you will still retain a very great deal of the earthly element in your soul. You have to learn to enter that heavenly state of consciousness whilst you are still here in a physical body; you have to work whilst you are in incarnation to develop these spiritual attributes and to use them for the blessing of mankind. This is a most important period in the world's history, and you are pioneers. You are called upon to fulfil a great mission. Whoever you are, you all have the same opportunity to bring through into manifestation on earth the divine aspect of life.

Whilst each individual must develop on its own lone path, it is never left alone. A paradox! While each of you is separate, each of you has your own particular line of development and initiation, and you are brought into a collective life, or brotherhood, through which you, in common with others there assembled, receive the benefit of the collective power and light drawn thither by the collective souls. Sooner or later the soul is made aware of the whole group. Up to that time it appears to travel alone at least in its own consciousness. The time arrives when the individual suddenly becomes aware of its fellowship with the *group*. This is of vital importance. The drawing together of the many into the group is governed purely by the karma of the individual. Those constituting the group meet not once, but in many lives. Thus you have heard us say that many of you have been together in a group, or brotherhood, similar to this. You forget, maybe; but that silent voice which successive initiations will enable you to hear will say to you: 'Yes, I remember, I know; I even yet do not fully remember, but I have a feeling'. Oh, how valuable are those feelings! The angels help human evolution through *feeling* . . . .

Therefore the soul preparing for initiation should recognise the needs of his brothers, become aware of the co-operation of the group soul. When initiation brings expansion of consciousness to the candidate, enabling him to become aware of his particular group, he no longer lives to himself, for himself, but recognises that every thought, every action, concerns not himself alone, but will inspire and help, or hurt or degrade (as the case may be) all his brothers in the group. Therefore the responsibility becomes very great. He is no longer free, so to speak. He never has been free, actually, but he thought himself alone. Now he is no longer free, because he is aware that he cannot injure any brother in his group without the whole group being affected, including himself. In very truth no man really can act to himself, or for himself. He may pride himself on isolation, but it is impossible to

---

injure another without injuring the self. The point we are trying to convey is that after initiation into this awareness of the group, the responsibility of the soul becomes vastly greater.

Most of you know a little of those whom we call our Elder Brethren, or the masters. Perhaps some of you have been brought into very close contact with these glorious beings, and you will know how beautiful they are. How have they attained to that degree of spiritual power and glory? Through the human life on earth; through self-discipline, self-control, service to their brother man; through allowing the divine will within them to rise and take possession of their lives. They bless through their divinity, through the Christ within shining forth amongst men.

Remember the purpose of life – it is not to escape from the earth and to idle away your time in a more beautiful place of thought or conscious being, but rather to perfect your ability to meet the everyday demands of life by bringing through into practical manifestation the beauty and har-mony of that heavenly state, and thus give the very finest service to your fellow men. It is that the God-consciousness within will expand into the perfection which lies within the mind of our Father–Mother God. For man was created in God's own image; the conception of the Perfect One is within the Trinity, is part of God. And you, my brother, my sister, *you* are that perfect conception of the child or son of God held within the mind of the Father–Mother. Meditate upon this, upon the holy three – God the Father, God the Mother, and you, the child . . . the very child of God, an aspect of that Trinity.

If, each day, you aspire to become in tune with the infinite, you will be developing the child of God, the Christ child in your heart. Men so sorely need that closer relationship with the Source of all life, the Father–Mother God, and when man's life on earth is built on an understanding of this relationship of child and parent, man and God, there will be no more suffering and sickness, chaos and war.

We would have you realise, my dear brethren, the power of the divinity within you. Don't let the worldly life weigh you down and crush you. Rise, my brother, my sister! Rise superior to the bondage of earth!

———

And the light shineth in darkness: and the darkness comprehended it not. The darkness is that of man, bound in physical matter, unconscious of the light of the divinity within.

There is another aspect of light and darkness we would like you to understand. We learnt in the temples of old that the right side of the body was the part of light. It was all light. The left side of the body was darkness. But this does not mean quite what you may think. The darkness of the left side indicated the invisible aspect of man. You probably know that in healing you give with your right hand – an outward symbol. You give the right hand of fellowship and goodwill. You receive with your left hand, the negative side of you, which is indicative of the invisible side. You absorb from the invisible with your left; you contact the world of matter with your right. Both light and darkness were together, one. This is another secret of the mysteries, perfect equilibrium – the perfect balancing of those two aspects of life.

You have read many times of the temple, which symbolises man's body, the place where the divine spirit resides. The two pillars, which support life, which support man's being, are the heart, the centre of love and wisdom; and the mind, which is the centre of power, of energy and will; and that which unites the two, the keystone of the arch, is the Christ spirit.

Let us also liken the two pillars in the temple to the dual soul, or the dual spirit, male and female, father and mother if you like, dual aspects of God; and when these two are wedded, when there is that perfect balance between heart and mind, or when there is a perfect mystical marriage, from that union there is born the holy child of God, Christ. We would suggest this as yet another esoteric interpretation of the im-maculate conception, the perfect blending of the intuition and the spiritual qualities of the mother with those of the father, the mind: and with this perfect blending, this perfect marriage within man's innermost being, the perfect Son of God, the perfect man, is born.

Let us bring this right down to the physi-cal plane; and what do we see in the world today? Chaos, cruelty, sorrow, terrible suf-fering? And why? What has brought this state of things to pass? Because humanity has starved for lack of understanding of the mother principle for many centuries. There has been domination, first by the body and then by the intellect or mind of man. Both have tended to imprison, if not slay, the divine mother principle, which is wisdom and love. In the future there must come, there will come, this illumination, this initiation, this expansion of spiritual awareness. You will see this mother aspect (not merely woman – we are speaking of divine principles) you will see this divine principle of the mother slowly but surely influencing the world. As a result there will be a much greater inflow of love and wisdom, a balancing of the power aspect which, by itself, brings destruction.

When the spirit of the mother moves in perfect balance with the father principle (which is the higher, the divine mind) there will be a return to sanity, to harmony, to happiness. We would say here that although we are not dealing wholly with the male and female aspects of mankind, nevertheless we speak very earnestly to women in particular, because they are the laggards in the work which has been put before them in this incarnation. We are not speaking merely of bearing children; a woman should be mother to the whole human race.

If every woman will stop and consider

her true mission, which is to express divine motherhood in the world through love and gentleness and wisdom, the attributes of the holy mother; if every man will realise his opportunity to express divine fatherhood – not by power and domination but by divine energy and will to help forward the evolution of the race, then will come that true balance between the two forces, which will raise mankind. The brain of man must be used, not for him to achieve power over his fellows but to understand and work in harmony with spiritual and physical law, and to bring through noble and fine inventions which will further help to evolve the soul of man. So much waits to come through when man can attune himself to the divine thought and become a ready channel.

We started by speaking of the symbol of the cross, which was a symbol of man well balanced, his head in the heaven and his feet upon earth. All must aspire to that perfect balance of life, so that the light of divinity shines in the darkness or in the unconsciousness of man, irradiating the life, bringing about complete and perfect illumination. Then, his term of service on earth finished, man will pass onward to fresh and more glorious experience. Every step of the journey must be taken, there are no short cuts; and you, my brethren, have been given the blessing of the knowledge that you do not take that journey alone. By your side is the companion of your spirit. Hand in hand with angels, or with the true companion of your soul, you walk the path from the unconsciousness or darkness of the human life into the glory and the light of the divine. Do not think that you cannot reach such a high state of consciousness. It is within you; the power of God is in you and raises you to the highest pinnacle of spiritual life. Follow that inner light. Bless you! Bless you!

❧

8

THE WAY OF A BROTHER

Brethren, we open our hearts to the inflow of the love, peace and power of our heavenly Father; to all that is good, pure and holy – wholesome, healthy. O Great White Spirit, we are thankful to Thee for the sustenance of our lives, for the joys which life brings. We are thankful too for its tests and trials, for its sorrows, for through these experiences our consciousness is opened to the glory of Thy heaven world, to the sweetness and beauty of Thy love. Thou knowest, O Lord, the need of all Thy children, who humbly pray that they may be receptive to Thy wisdom, which Thou dost speak to them according to Thy laws. May the rays of the Great White Light, the Christos, bless this communion.

Amen.

DEAR BRETHREN (and we call you brethren because you are all held within the love of the Great White Spirit, in Whom we all live and have our being): dear brethren, we speak from the world of spirit and would reach not only your minds but your hearts – reach to your innermost spirit.

Some of you would like to know more about the Brotherhood of the Light, the White Brotherhood; or, as some of you know it, the Christ Star Brotherhood. This Brotherhood is not of course limited to Christians, as you understand the meaning of the word. Brothers of the Great White Light have manifested in all religions during all time. But apart from the great brotherhood of human souls, we want you to think also about the brotherhood of all life – consisting of human beings, the animal kingdom, the nature world, the spirit world, the angelic kingdoms. Think also about all the natural elements, each having attached to it an angelic being, or beings, concerned with its particular element. Do you remember how our beloved Francis of Assisi refers to Brother Air, Sister Water, Brother Fire, Brother Sun, as though they were to him part of the one great family? Brother Francis was himself one of a great number of highly-evolved souls which have come to earth from time immemorial to help mankind to become aware of this infinite universal life.

Although the Brotherhood has never been restricted to orthodox Christianity, all are, of course, brothers in the Christ Light.* In that sense they must be Christian brothers; but when you study the inner records of past races you will find that quiet and secret brotherhoods have existed in many countries – in the East, in the West, in the North and in the South, throughout all time. Always they have been established in remote places where the brothers lived according to what they understood to be the law of God. Before any candidate was accepted and initiated into the inner work of the brotherhood, he had to face severe tests and trials – tests in his everyday experience, and also tests of the quality of his love for God, of his devotion to the brotherhood, of his strength of purpose, and concerning his motives.

The reason why the brothers had to endure such tests was that they had to prove themselves ready and able to use certain innate powers which initiation would stimulate. Initiation was therefore looked upon as a very serious and important step.

Now there are dangers on this path of

*i.e., the universal divine light.

———

91

spiritual service. We do not want to scare anyone, only to make you strong in wisdom. Nevertheless, understand that when man's inner eye is opened and inner powers are stimulated, he is going to meet certain dangers. For this reason the brothers in ancient days were tested for courage, wisdom, soundness of mind and healthfulness of body. They had to live wisely, physically. The brethren had to learn to discipline themselves, to control the desires and instincts of the body; to eat pure food, consciously to breathe the pure air, to cleanse the body daily with sweet Sister Water, to think rightly. They had to prove they could perform all the disciplinary rites required of them in their service. So you see, it was not an easy path.

But it is not God who keeps man outside the heaven which can be found in the heart of the brotherhood; it is man himself. Within you lies all that you will need during your journey through the many lives leading upward and onward to the golden world of God. But if it were easy for man to enter the promised land, if he did not have to discipline and train himself, he would never realise its radiance. All scriptures tell this

———

symbolic story of the growth and unfoldment of man's soul; of his breaking away
from the land of Egypt, his leaving the
flesh-pots, or temptations of the flesh. In
Pharaoh's court there was worship of the
body and the senses. At certain stages man
goes through this worldly phase. Then a call
comes to him, and he finds a leader, such as
Moses was to the Israelites, who explains
how he can leave behind the negative aspects
of life, and arise and follow his master to the
Promised Land. In this way Moses led the
children of Israel – who had been slaves to
Pharaoh, or to the physical and material life,
and were searching for 'Isra', for the Great
Sun – out of the bondage of Egypt.

First, you will remember, they wandered
in the wilderness and became very discon-
tented because everything proved hard and
difficult. Compare this with your own
experience, those of you who have heard the
call, and note that you also came up against
rather dreary work and felt chained to tasks
you did not like, so you couldn't get away
from your wilderness. Now Moses heard the
voice of God; he climbed the mountain (he
was raised in consciousness to a state of
spiritual ecstasy) and received from his

———

Creator stones upon which was written the law of God. When he came down, his people had set up and were worshipping a golden calf (again, materiality). So shocked was he that he dashed the stones to the ground and they were broken. Again he was called up the mountain and received a fresh statement of the law. We interpret this to mean that man can only be given what he can understand and accept at a given time. He cannot receive more than he can comprehend. You may notice that you too only get a little at a time, and sometimes you may be tempted to think, 'Oh, I know all this! Now I want the next step'. But you see, you cannot have a new revelation until you have not only accepted but absorbed into your very being the simpler teaching. You must thoroughly absorb and live it. It is no good reading books; it is no good listening to talks. You must *feel*. You must know and feel truth deep within your heart. When you have really *become* that light through service to your brother man, then you are ready for the unfolding of deeper mysteries.

So will you, my dear young brethren, be patient and keep on keeping on? You cannot rush the gates of heaven; you have to keep on patiently, perhaps at a very humdrum task, and may feel sometimes that you could do much better than your brother if only you were in your brother's place. But if you could, then you would have been given that place.

We know how every brother feels, we know how sometimes the way seems tedious and difficult. You think that if we could present you with something exciting, even thrilling, oh, how attractive everything would be! But there might be little flavour in the fruit you covet. A brother must see clearly the choice between the material and the spiritual life, for he cannot serve two masters. He must face truth. So if you long with all your heart and soul and mind to follow truth, then whoever you are, what-ever your service, whether it be purely spiri-tual or whether it lies in the material world (and you can give great service at that level, remember), are you prepared to give up everything which has been desirable in the latter sense and follow the one path? You are? Very well! Then you are accepted, but do you know what this means? It means unremitting work. But there is compensa-tion, and the compensation lies in the joy inherent in that service, the ineffable joy which comes to the servant of God. Then he feels no regret; possessions mean nothing when he has the greatest possession of all, the joy of being able to serve God and his brother man.

You may think that we paint too gloomy a picture. Not so at all. Look at the great ones of all time and see that their life was ever a life of service. Do you remember how weary Jesus became at times, and yet his disciples pleaded, 'Oh, there is a man here who needs you', or 'The multitude have come from afar and would hear you speak'. and instantly Jesus would forget his weariness and go forth again to minister.

This is what we mean by unremitting service. You will see, therefore, why you must necessarily be very sturdy and strong in body and soul, and in your character. If you were not healthy you would crumple up, and just when your people were in the greatest need you would be unable to serve them.*

*We feel that White Eagle here speaks of an ideal of health, and particularly of *inner* vitality. He has many times stressed how those who suffer debilitating illness in fact give great service to their fellow men and women.

Because of the great tests, and the burden laid upon those who would serve, they have to be strictly trained and disciplined.

The true brother seeks to live healthily, which means in holiness and purity. He seeks to live lovingly and joyously; he lives to radiate the light and beauty, the love and truth of God, and he loves all creatures. He could not knowingly inflict pain. All life is one and all life is governed by the divine law, love; and every hurt, every cruelty inflicted upon life in any form, man himself will have to suffer because actually he has inflicted it upon himself. Once recognise, once comprehend that you are all part of an infinite, universal life, and you will know that you cannot hurt *anything*, because it is in you and you are in the whole of it.

At present your consciousness may be limited, but it will expand in the course of possibly many incarnations. Spiritual unfoldment must of necessity be slow, but the reward for this spiritual unfoldment and service is beyond all description. *Eye hath not seen, nor ear heard, the things which God hath prepared!* Oh dear brethren, we long to help you onward and upward, and although the way may sometimes seem stony and you may become weary, you will all the way receive that ineffable sweetness and happiness which will make all the experiences of your life more than worthwhile.

Every individual soul has its work to do. None can do the work of another. Each must do his own work. Therefore we say, accept it, my child. Pray to the Great White Spirit that you may not fail in any task laid before you.

The Brotherhood would leave you with their love, their peace; and they remind you that although you may have to work hard, work can be joyous too. Try to understand that although the spiritual life may seem difficult, it brings heavenly blessings. God never owes anyone anything, He always pays His debts. The labourer is worthy of his hire, it is said – in Masonic language, the brother is sent to the temple to receive just wages. If we were to ask you to testify whether you had ever been sent to the temple and received just wages for your work, many of you could raise your hands and testify: 'Aye. Aye. Aye. We have had just wage'.

Now let us raise our hearts to the infinite Spirit, our heavenly Father and divine and earthly

Mother, to the elder brethren and the great angels of life. We see them in the golden light of Christ the Son, and feel the blessing of these golden rays pouring down upon us, filling our hearts now with joy and thankfulness . . .

Amen.

━━━━

ଔୀଶ

9

SAYINGS OF THE GENTLE BROTHER

Tolerance, Meekness, Love

BELOVED BRETHREN, we bring to each one of you tender love and a great understanding of your difficulties and of your work and ideals and aspirations. Remember always that you do not walk the path of earth life alone, for always your teacher in spirit, who will never fail you, is by your side. When you pray for understanding, it will come to you; but it will come to you first in your heart mind, not in the mind of earth. This is why we try to bring home to you all the realisation of the light of God, the light which is called the Christ, in all humanity: the light in your heart which makes you sons and daughters of God, and speaks through your love for your fellow men and women, your love towards life and all the circumstances of life.

Look out upon the world and your companions without envy, without judgment, without criticism – only with love, recognising that you are all on a similar path, that you all need one another. You cannot judge another soul, no matter how clearly you think you can see his faults or her weaknesses, for you cannot see the burden of karma he carries, nor what lies behind his actions. Look upon all people with understanding, knowing that all have their secret heartaches, their weariness of the flesh – all, unknowingly, are searching for gold. At the lower levels the gold is a substance, hard metal. At higher levels it is spiritual awareness.

May love inspire your life at every turn. This is your freewill choice. But remember that your fellow man has the same freewill. Do not force your way into the heart of your brother, but stand by him with love in your heart, so that he may take, if he is ready to receive.

The lesson of discrimination is important, for your brother has the choice to respond to your love and to the love of God which will heal him and help him to find happiness; or he may resolutely turn his back upon that light and go in the opposite direction. You cannot interfere, for this is his choice. This lesson of discrimination and of man's freewill choice is very subtle, but you must understand it; and with the understanding will come tolerance, meekness, love.

The Real and the Unreal

THE MASTER would have you give way in little things that are unimportant. Give way to each other on little things. Be not attentive of yourself. But be very strong for right when right is a matter of principle. Also be sure not to make mountains out of molehills. Get a clear and balanced perspective so that you see all things truly. If you follow this rule you will be much helped in daily life and you will be able to bring greater blessing to others.

Many details can cause irritation, but such details are usually trivialities which do not matter. Learn to distinguish between the real and the unreal, the important and the unimportant, and in this way you will grow big of heart and of soul. A great soul houses no smallness or pettiness.

———

This message is addressed to all and it comes from the Master himself. It is sent with love and understanding of how you think and feel, far beyond your own understanding of yourself. He blesses you and says that he is thankful that you seek his help, that you turn your face towards Him – only his Father in Heaven can know how thankful he is.

There comes a vision, a picture of the Master kneeling . . . He draws close to each one who loves him. He bathes your feet . . . can you, in your hearts, do likewise to each other? Can you kneel at your brother's feet and thus minister to him (even in thought) unless you have a spirit of deep and true humility? When you can feel and can continue to feel thus towards each other, you will grow very near the Master . . . and he to you.

The Transmutation of Karma

IT IS so easy to judge the actions of others, but do try to refrain from judgment, for as you condemn others, so you condemn yourself. Strive to be tolerant and to give from your heart the gentle spirit of the master

———

soul. Jesus the Christ is a master soul, man made perfect; and this highly evolved and perfected soul incarnated in order to reveal to individual man what he could himself attain to if he followed the simple, gentle way of the Christ.

Forgive, my children, forgive. Whatever is in your heart, however hard you may feel towards any soul, possibly with justification according to material standards, pray to forgive, as Jesus taught in his simple prayer: *Forgive us our trespasses, as we forgive those who trespass against us.* Do you not realise that in forgiving others, you are releasing yourselves? So long as you sit in harsh judgment on your fellows, refusing to forgive, you bring that same judgment upon yourself, for life is ruled by spiritual law: as you give, so you receive. But as soon as you feel forgiveness in your own heart, you release yourself from the bondage of your karma.

Karma is transmuted when you learn to think and act from the spirit, with love.

Jesus pointed the way. He lived to demonstrate this profound truth, because he was all compassion. He looked into the soul of his friends, of those who drew close to him; he saw their suffering and he saw even more than present suffering; he saw their whole life, the karma of the individual, and what made them act as they did. And so Jesus had compassion. He forgave so much. He showed the Way.

Forgiveness is often difficult, my children; but as soon as forgiveness comes into the heart, there comes release of the spirit; the soul that has been in bondage and perhaps stretched upon the cross of suffering no longer suffers.

Learn to look into the heart, to love – and to forgive.

Simplicity

THE MASTER looks for humility in his disciples – he looks for the simple soul, the faithful soul, the loving soul . . . and if you start with these qualities, you will give the finest that is within you and you will be used according to your capacity.

You will be tried and tested, but accept these tests with humble thankfulness. The lower mind will tempt you; it will pull you down, cause you to doubt, cause you to feel weary. But don't give way to this temptation, for it is the lower mind which tempts you. The higher mind, through which we work, will bring you joy and assurance, and will cause your whole being to pulsate with happiness.

Nothing is too beautiful for you to believe; and if your lower mind and so-called reason tempt you to dismiss our words, remember it is the mind of the tempter, of darkness. The destructive force always wants to hold back, to delay progress. The higher mind, the spiritual mind, always encourages you to see the good, the true, the beautiful. The lower mind encourages you to see with a pessimistic vision, but between over-optimism and over-pessimism there is a steady level of balanced thought. Your symbol, the star, is to teach you balance, balance between the two forces, between heaven and earth. Hold always the positive thought, good thought, God thought; and see the vision before you of the unfailing, manifesting light of the Creator.

And do not forget we are with you, looking on with great love, sometimes with humour. Oh yes! We have a great sense of humour, you know! – but kindly humour. And we suggest that you too encourage that sense of humour. Keep your eyes twinkling – it will be a great help.

Never look back! Never look down! Always look up! Look up! And from the star which shines above you will receive all that you need, spiritually, mentally, physically and materially. You cannot set your vision too high.

I lift mine eyes

THERE ARE times during earthly life when the body gets heavy to carry and the path becomes wearisome. We would like to help you at such times, and we can help you if you allow us to. This means that you should turn your thoughts away from the bondage of earth and the physical body, and look into the heights, to the mountain tops, where there is peace and strength and life eternal.

When you are raised to that higher plane of spiritual realisation, how small your material cares seem to you! Indeed they do not seem real at all, and all physical disability recedes into the background. Now if you could always maintain your contact with the spiritual level of life you would find that your earthly life would become healthy, holy, harmonious. We know that it is very easy for us to talk like this, but you also know, brethren, that when on rare occasions you do make that true contact with the life of spirit all inharmony and pain fall away from you and you live for that brief moment in an ecstasy of spiritual happiness. This is perhaps what the Master Jesus was trying to teach you when he said, *I and my Father are one. The Father that dwelleth in me, he doeth the works.* It is not beyond the power of any soul to touch that realm of harmony and perfectness.

Now, my children, when you are faced with problems and perplexities, seek first the kingdom of heaven, the kingdom of God, seek your daily contact with the Source of your spiritual and physical being. Take your problems into your own private chapel in the world of spirit on the etheric plane. Create in imagination your own private chapel – you can make it very beautiful – and then kneel in simplicity before the shrine and ask, and your Father will hear you and the light will shine in your heart; the light will reveal truth to you and show you what to do. Follow the true light, not the light of your own desire. Lay your desires on one side and seek in simplicity and in truth. The light will guide you. Be strong in the light.

I AM the Way

YOU DO NOT yet fully realise how important is the continual effort towards good thought, God thought; for this is not only building the temple, the spiritual body, the celestial body of the individual, but it is refining the physical body also. Some of you feel a certain complacency in the thought that life is law; you feel that you are in a sense an automaton, held in this law of nature, and cannot help yourself. This is not true. Every person has within him the God power; and as you learn to use this power of God in you, so you are recreating the life that you live and also creating a more beautiful world around you.

If you think of someone whose life is controlled by positive good thought, of a life directed from the heart, from the Son or Christ spirit, you know that such a life is well-ordered, peaceful, harmonious, happy. Nothing disturbs it. This law and order works gently, beautifully and harmoniously

---

throughout the life, making all things new, all things perfect. On the other hand, the life under the domination of negative or destructive thoughts is ungoverned, uncontrolled, unhappy, inharmonious, is full of chaos.

But as Jesus said upon the cross, *Father, forgive them; for they know not what they do.* It is ignorance which brings this chaos. Ignorance is itself chaotic, undisciplined darkness. When once the soul earnestly seeks knowledge or understanding, then that soul is set upon a path which will lead to the temple of wisdom and knowledge.

The man who follows the path of light enters into the fullness of eternal life, not in some life far away in some dim future, but here and now. He enters into a deep understanding of the power of the God life within him, which can control his mind and emotions, and which can sustain itself by drawing upon the eternal light of God; and uses it for the blessing and healing of all mankind. This power Jesus himself demonstrated in his life, and is what he was referring to when he said: *I AM the way, the truth and the life.* Jesus, or the Christ through the lips of Jesus, was speaking of that life which

---

every human soul inherits; that life which is the spiritual sun beyond all physical manifestation; of that spiritual glory which man can receive into his own being and which can transform his life from darkness to light.

Be True to Yourself

REMEMBER always the quiet, pure and true contact within the sanctuary of your own being. Be true to your own self, your own spirit, and in being true to yourself you will be true also to God and the universal Brotherhood.

Many people on earth and many sources on the etheric plane will delight in trying to pull you away from that still centre of truth. Do not be pulled; but hold fast to the pure vision of goodness, truth and love. Be watchful and alert and do not be beguiled by false values. It is easy to slip off the straight path.

Having offered yourselves in sincerity and faith to the work of God and the Brotherhood, remember that *the starting point of this work is yourself*. We can only give you principles or signposts and you must work in the simplest way on each problem as it presents itself to you in your daily life, according to the principles given you. We do not come to relieve you of your opportunities. We come to bring you power, wisdom and love. We of the Brotherhood do not expect more than you can give at your present stage on the path, but every brother can, at given times, seek attunement with the Eternal Light, can commune with God, can worship God. This you do in ways most harmonious to you personally. There are many rays reaching from the periphery to the centre, but whichever ray your soul is on, reach forward to God, the heart from which the life-blood flows. The Brethren in the Temple sit in a circle, hand in hand, their hearts reaching out to the heart in the centre. This is truly the round table of the Knights of the Temple. You are all striving to become true knights.

Your Master teaches you in a very simple way the rules of the Brotherhood and you must endeavour to understand and apply these rules to your life.

Try to distinguish between the limitations of personality and the limitlessness of God's life. Live to send out light, and this means seeing good in everything. If it doesn't appear to be good, then *make it good*. It will become good because all the things work together for good. All will be good and will come right if you centre your vision upon God, because God is ever evolving, creating, bringing good out of evil, order out of chaos, light out of darkness.

Release from Darkness

LET US meditate, being conscious of the light of the Christ generating from our heart and enveloping us. We feel a complete relaxation as we are bathed in the Christ Light . . . We are nothing – yet we *know that we are a flame within the eternal fire.*

Of what should we be most conscious in the heavenly world? Light – the sun. Yet in heaven are lesser lights – those of the angels round the throne, each representative of countless hosts of beings, all vibrating to their particular ray of life. Each lifestream is linked in the heavens to other worlds; and we as human beings receive direct power and influence from one angel in particular, and in general from all of these vast hosts.

———

Within this life we live and have our being; this is the power, the wisdom and the love in which we are encompassed. And yet bodily we remain in shadow because we are clothed in the darkness of the earth. But no man need for ever remain a prisoner; it only requires the will to aspire and so to know the wisdom of the divine – and the prisoner is free!

And so we ascend in spirit, and being raised as on to a hillside we then step forth into a life heavenly in its beauty and are encompassed by a heavenly concourse. We are conscious of the perfect proportion and exactitude of life: we become conscious of colour – shades, mists, clouds, volumes of exquisite colour, perfectly blended, inter-penetrating and taking form. All the heavens are filled with colour and light, since colour and light are the substances used in the formation or creation of differing forms of life. We may become conscious of music – delicate, gentle, sweet music beyond all description – which may swell in grand cres-cendo to embrace the great universal music of all creation. And we know that we are part of this grand orchestra.

_____

Faith

AMID THE apparent chaos of human blunders, you must never lose your faith in the love and wisdom of the Great Architect of the Universe. We have already impressed upon you the power of faith – if you had faith even as a grain of mustard seed, said Jesus, you could move mountains. Behind all occult law lies the power of faith.

Will you also remember that in your human life it is desirable for you to have a flexible attitude of mind? We mean by this that it is impossible to bind or limit truth. It is not wise to say 'Lo, here is truth; lo, there is truth'; but rather feel that everywhere lies truth. And if human life or human contacts fall short of the ideal which you have set, remember that your ideal may be a false, an incomplete ideal; and be ready to lay it aside, and see truth working through all the experiences of life. Never be too rigid; and remember also to judge no man. *Hath no man condemned thee? Neither do I condemn thee.* We have reached that stage of being wherein we feel only love and gentleness towards life, we begin to lose the sense of separation – for there is no separation in love.

———

Then there comes to the soul that wonderful interpenetration, that blending of the rays of colour, the rays of the rainbow blending into the one ray which is the pure white light. We pray that in your group work, your brotherhood work, you may experience, if only fleetingly, that beauty of the blending of the soul of you all, so that you are as one soul, one ray of pure white light. There is no separation in love, there is no condemnation nor irritation, but power, joy, ecstasy even; and you know that God is All. You know that God is in you and you are in God. You know there can be no error in God; you know that if you have patience and faith and trust all your problems will be worked out. You know that God is Love.

SUBJECT INDEX

THE WHITE EAGLE PUBLISHING TRUST, which publishes and distributes the White Eagle teaching, is part of the wider work of the White Eagle Lodge, an undenominational Christian church founded in 1936 to give practical expression to the White Eagle teaching. Here men and women may come to learn the reason for their life on earth and how to serve and live in harmony with the whole brotherhood of life, visible and invisible, in health and happiness.

Readers wishing to know more of the work of the White Eagle Lodge may write to the General Secretary, The White Eagle Lodge, New Lands, Brewells Lane, Liss, Hampshire, England GU33 7HY (tel. 0730 893300) or can call at The White Eagle Lodge, 9 St Mary Abbots Place, Kensington, London W8 6LS (tel. 01-603 7914). In the Americas our representative is at P.O. Box 930, Montgomery, Texas 77356, and in Australasia at Willomee, P.O. Box 225, Maleny, Queensland 4552.